The BADGERS GO CAMPING

by Andrew Willett
illustrated by Tim Robinson

MODERN CURRICULUM PRESS
Pearson Learning Group

MW01046352

his is a picture of everyone who went on the Badger Scouts' annual camping trip. My name is Ed, and the other kids are Erika, Becky, Todd, and Paul. Erika's dad and mom, Mr. and Mrs. George, came along to keep an eye on us. He's the assistant scoutmaster. Usually there are about twelve other Badgers in our troop, but this year almost everybody had the chicken pox.

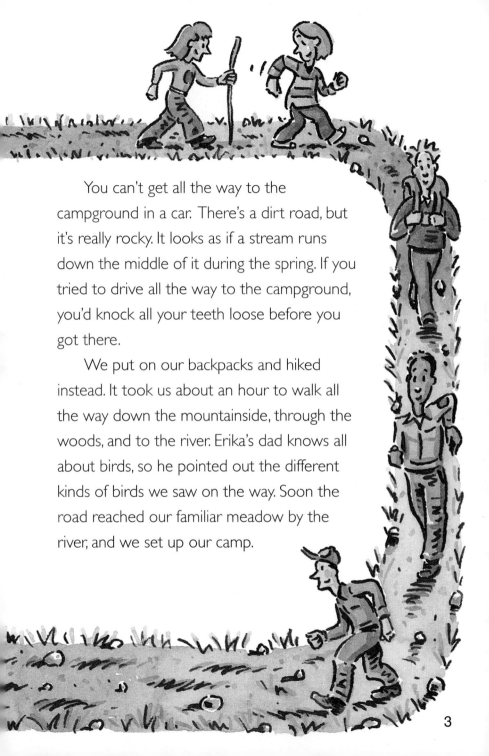

You can't get all the way to the campground in a car. There's a dirt road, but it's really rocky. It looks as if a stream runs down the middle of it during the spring. If you tried to drive all the way to the campground, you'd knock all your teeth loose before you got there.

We put on our backpacks and hiked instead. It took us about an hour to walk all the way down the mountainside, through the woods, and to the river. Erika's dad knows all about birds, so he pointed out the different kinds of birds we saw on the way. Soon the road reached our familiar meadow by the river, and we set up our camp.

The weather reports had said that the skies would be clear that weekend, so we decided to leave the tent in the car and sleep out under the stars. We were all excited at the idea. In the city, the lights are always too bright to see many stars. The Badgers love the chance to go someplace really dark, where we can see the sky well.

When we reached the campsite, the first thing we did was go for a swim. Mountain rivers are clear, sparkling, and much colder than you think they will be. After all, you're swimming in melted snow from far up on the mountain's peak.

But when you get cold, there's nothing better than lying on a rock in the sun, warming up, and not hearing any city traffic. All you hear is the wind, the river, and the birds.

When the afternoon started to turn into evening, we gathered some firewood. There are always old dry branches on the ground in the woods around the meadow. Dried-out wood is easy to ignite and makes for great campfires. We broke up some branches into smaller sticks. What we couldn't break with our hands and feet, Mr. George chopped up with a hatchet.

Once the fire was burning, we ate our dinner, which we cooked ourselves. We sang a few songs around the fire and told spooky stories. We watched some bats flutter quietly across the clearing, eating moths and other insects.

And then we went to bed. The fire crackled as it smoldered and died out, and the sky was dusted with a million stars that glittered like sugar. It was the most peaceful thing I had ever seen.

We woke up early the next morning, not long after the sun rose. Everybody had slept well except for Todd, who said that a rock had somehow sprouted underneath him during the night. We ate breakfast, brushed our teeth, and went for a walk around the clearing. Erika's mom and dad helped us look for animals in the meadow, and we tried to list all the animals we could see or that we could tell lived there.

Then Becky spoke up. "Um, do you hear a car?" Becky has the best ears of anybody I know. Soon we could hear the car too. "It sounds like it's coming down the road!"

"Who would try to drive down here?" I asked. It seemed like a strange idea to all of us.

But then an old camper came bouncing into view, and our weekend in the woods took a surprising turn. We were about to meet the Dinns.

We couldn't believe that somebody had driven a camper down the bumpy road. We really couldn't believe that this old camper had survived the journey. It was dented and dusty and looked as if it were ready to fall apart. We saw a couple of people in the front seats. They waved to us as they drove into the clearing. Then they turned and headed toward the trees on the far side, just past a bend in the river.

"I guess we won't be the only campers here this weekend," said Erika's mom. "It's a big meadow, though, and it looks as though they'll be camping a distance away from us. I doubt we'll bother them."

"Oh, hey, look out!" said Paul, but it was too late. We could see that the camper had backed into a young pine tree and knocked it over. Its roots stuck into the air. I started to worry about our new neighbors. Before long, my worst fears would come true.

The first thing the couple did after they parked was pull a boxy thing like a little car engine out of the back of the camper. Soon a sound like an angry motorcycle cut across the clearing.

"What on Earth? Is that a generator? Why would they need—"

Erika's dad never got to finish his question because we found out right away why they wanted a generator. They plugged a big radio into it, and soon the clearing was filled with loud music. Very loud music. Birds started flying up out of the meadow.

"Becky, have you got the sandwiches?" asked Mrs. George. "Good. Let's take that hike now. Maybe they'll be tired of the noise when we get back." But when we came back that afternoon, the music was still going strong.

"Why don't you guys go for a swim?" said Mr. George. "Maybe I can get those folks to make a little less noise."

We went swimming. The river was still cold. Suddenly Paul noticed two bright yellow things floating down the river. They were two bags of potato chips! "They must belong to those people over there. Let's go take them back. Besides, I want to meet them," he said.

"Why, thank you!" said the woman at the campsite when we gave her the bags. The music had stopped. The generator was still roaring, but as far as we could tell they weren't using it for anything. "You know, we went for a picnic down by the water while you were on your hike, and I dropped my groceries. I was so sorry to lose those chips! Aren't you sweet to find them for us! My name's Mrs. Dinn. That's Mr. Dinn in the camper. If you need anything, you come find us."

"Did you smell the gasoline over by the Dinns' camper?" asked Becky later as we ate our dinner by the fire. The sun had finally set. The Dinns' generator was still running.

"How could you smell anything with all that exhaust coming from the generator?" Todd answered.

"No, I mean it. I saw an empty gas can on its side. I'll bet they kicked it over by mistake. It smelled bad over there."

"Well, at least they turned off the music," said Erika's father. "I don't think they realize that quiet is one of the good things about the wilderness."

Suddenly the meadow was full of light. Now what?

We turned toward the camper. The Dinns were running a long string of bright light bulbs between their camper and the trees.

Erika was furious. "This is the woods. It's supposed to get dark at night. That's the whole idea!"

"And look at all that smoke from their fire," said Paul. "They've chopped up that tree they knocked over! They'll never really get it to ignite. You can't burn green wood like that."

Mr. George just put his head in his hands and groaned. Mrs. George shook her head.

The bright lights stayed on after we went
to bed. It was harder to see the stars, but if
you didn't look over in the Dinns' direction,
you were okay. There were funny popping
noises too.

I sat up. Becky was looking toward the
lights with her mouth open. "They have a bug
zapper over there! What are they thinking?
There are more bugs in this meadow than
they could zap in a month!"

The lights and sounds kept us up for
what seemed like forever. Then the generator
sputtered and died, and the meadow became
dark and quiet at last. The stars came back, and
everyone slept. The next morning we woke up
when the sun rose. We were all sleepier than
we had been the morning before.

"I'm not kidding," said Todd, rubbing a sore
shoulder. "I think the rocks burrowed under
my sleeping bag while I was sleeping. I'm sure
these weren't here last night."

We all took a swim right away, hoping that
the cold water would wake us up. It worked.
When we heard the unhappy cries coming
from the Dinns' camp, we went running.

"Oh, no! What are we going to do now? Our trip is ruined!"

Mrs. Dinn was very upset. Mr. Dinn was holding a gasoline can over the generator, but nothing was pouring out into the generator's gas tank.

"What's the matter, Mrs. Dinn?" asked Erika.

"Mr. Dinn left our gasoline can open yesterday, and he must have knocked it over. It's all gone! How will we run our generator? What will we do without power for our radio? And our bug zapper?"

"Well, you're welcome to spend the day with the Badger Scouts," said Mrs. George. She had crossed the meadow to find out what was going on. "We camp without electricity all the time."

"Aren't you Scouts clever!" said Mrs. Dinn.

We had just returned from a day-long hike through the woods. Erika's dad had tested us all on the birds and animals we saw along the way. "I had no idea there were so many different kinds of birds out here. Why, Mr. Dinn and I hardly ever see any birds when we go camping!"

We looked at each other. We all had a good idea why the Dinns never saw any birds, but we didn't say anything.

Mr. George picked up the hatchet. "Hey, Scouts, it's nearly evening. How about finding some firewood?"

"A campfire! With the Badger Scouts!" Mrs. Dinn exclaimed. "How wonderful! And I'll bet you know how to build a good fire. The fire we built last night wouldn't burn. It just smoldered. It was so sad."

"Come with us, Mrs. Dinn," said Paul. "Tonight you'll earn your Badger Scouts fire-building badge."

Mrs. Dinn turned out to be a fast learner when it came to fire building.

That night was our last night in the woods, and the Badgers and the Dinns shared a feast. Mrs. Dinn sang harmony to our campfire songs in her high, warbling voice. And Mr. Dinn turned out to know some great stories. He told funny ones and spooky ones until we were all too tired to stay up.

As the Dinns stood up to go back across the meadow to their camper, Mrs. Dinn turned on a small flashlight.

"Wait, dear," said Mr. Dinn. "Turn the light back off. Look at all the stars! Have you ever seen anything so lovely?"

We all sat in silence for a long while, looking up at the sky. "It's wonderful," Mrs. Dinn said. She was right.